PowerKids Readers:

The Bilingual Library of the United States of America™

Bilingual Edition
English/Spanish
Edición bilingüe

MAINE

JOSÉ MARÍA OBREGÓN

TRADUCCIÓN AL ESPA—OL: MARÍA CRISTINA BRUSCA

The Rosen Publishing Group's
PowerKids Press™ & Editorial Buenas Letras™
New York

Published in 2006 by The Rosen Publishing Group, Inc.
29 East 21st Street, New York, NY 10010

First Edition

Book Design: Albert B. Hanner
Photo Credits: Cover © George H. H. Huey/Corbis; p. 5 © Joseph Sohm; ChromoSohm Inc./Corbis; p. 7 © 2002 GeoAtlas; pp. 9, 31 (Harbor) © Royalty-Free/Corbis; p. 11 © W. Cody/Corbis; pp. 13, 15, 31 (Rockefeller) © Bettmann/Corbis; p. 17 © Fine Art Photographic Library/Corbis; p. 19 © Bob Krist/Corbis; p. 21 © Yogi, Inc./Corbis; pp. 23, 31 (Tyler) © Reuters/Corbis; pp. 25, 30 (Capital) © Jeff Greenberg/Index Stock Imagery, Inc.; pp. 26, 30 (White Pinecone and Tassel) by Albert Hanner; p. 30 (Chickadee) © Arthur Morris/Corbis; p. 30 (Pine Tree State, Eastern White Pine) © Richard Hamilton Smith/Corbis; p. 31 (Dix) © Corbis; p. 31 (Longfellow) © Hulton-Deutsch Collection/Corbis; p. 31 (Hamlin) © Medford Historical Society Collection/Corbis; p. 31 (King) © Seth Joel/Corbis; p. 31 (Submarine) © Steve Kaufman/Corbis

Library of Congress Cataloging-in-Publication Data

Obregón, José María, 1963–
Maine / José María Obregón ; traducción al español, María Cristina Brusca.— 1st ed.
p. cm. — (The bilingual library of the United States of America) Includes text in English and Spanish.
Includes bibliographical references and index.
ISBN 1-4042-3084-X (library binding)
1. Maine–Juvenile literature. I. Brusca, María Cristina. II. Title. III. Series.
F19.3.O27 2006
974.1—dc22

2005008330

Manufactured in the United States of America

Due to the changing nature of Internet links, Editorial Buenas Letras has developed an online list of Web sites related to the subject of this book. This site is updated regularly. Please use this link to access the list:

http://www.buenasletraslinks.com/ls/maine

Contents

Contenido

Welcome to Maine

These are the flag and seal of the state of Maine. The seal has a red banner with the state motto, *Dirigo*. It means "I direct" or "I lead." A motto is a saying.

Bienvenidos a Maine

Estos son la bandera y el escudo de Maine. El escudo tiene una banda roja con el lema del estado, *Dirigo*. Esto quiere decir "Yo guío" o "Yo dirijo". Un lema expresa una idea.

Maine Flag and State Seal

Bandera y escudo de Maine

Maine Geography

Maine borders the state of New Hampshire and the country of Canada. It also borders the Atlantic Ocean. The town of Sail Rock in Maine is the easternmost point in the United States.

Geografía de Maine

Maine linda con el estado de Nuevo Hampshire y con el país de Canadá. También está limitado por el océano Atlántico. El pueblo de Sail Rock es el punto situado más al este en los Estados Unidos.

Map of Maine

Mapa de Maine

Maine also borders the Atlantic Ocean. The state has more than 3,500 miles (5,633 km) of coastline with sandy beaches, bays, and harbors. Maine also has more than 2,000 islands off its coast.

Las costas de Maine bordean el océano Atlántico. El estado tiene más de 3,500 millas (5,633 km) de costa, con playas, bahías y puertos. Maine tiene también más de 2,000 islas cerca de sus costas.

Lighthouse in Mount Desert Island, Maine

Faro en la Isla Mount Desert, Maine

Maine is known as the Pine Tree State. This is because most of the state is covered with forest. This is more than any other state in the United States. Pine trees are found in all of Maine's forests.

Maine es conocido como el Estado del Pino. Se le llama así porque la mayoría del estado está cubierto de bosques. Maine tiene más bosques que cualquiera de los otros estados de los Estados Unidos. Todos los bosques de Maine tienen pinos.

Forest in Acadia National Park

Bosque en el Parque Nacional Acadia

Maine History

Native American tribes have been living in Maine since 500 B.C. Four Native American nations still live in Maine today. These are the Passamaquoddy, the Penobscot, the Micmac, and the Maliseet.

Historia de Maine

Varias tribus de nativos americanos han vivido en Maine desde el año 500 a.C. Cuatro de estas naciones indígenas siguen viviendo en Maine. Estas son los Passamaquoddy, Penobscot, Micmac y Maliseet.

A Family of the Penobscot Nation

Una familia de la nación Penobscot

In 1524, Giovanni da Verrazano became the first European to visit Maine. Verrazano claimed the land for France. Maine belonged to France until 1763.

En 1524, Giovanni da Verrazano fue el primer europeo en visitar Maine. Verrazano reclamó la tierra para Francia. Maine perteneció a Francia hasta 1763.

Giovanni da Verrazano

Maine was part of the Massachusetts colony. In 1775, the colonies wanted to separate from the British. War broke out between the British and the colonies. This war is known as the American Revolution.

Maine formó parte de la colonia de Massachusetts. En 1775, las colonias quisieron separarse de Gran Bretaña. Esto hizo estallar una guerra entre los británicos y las colonias. Esta guerra se conoce como la Guerra de Independencia.

A British Ship During the Battle of Falmouth Harbor, Maine

Barco británico durante la Batalla de Falmouth Harbor, en Maine

Living in Maine

Rockland, Maine, is known as the lobster capital of the world. Every summer the city celebrates Lobsterfest. Visitors from all over the country come to Rockland to eat lobster and take part in fun games.

La vida en Maine

Rockland, Maine, es conocida como la capital mundial de la langosta. Todos los veranos, la ciudad celebra el Festival de la Langosta. Visitantes de todo el país llegan a Rockland para comer langosta y participar en juegos muy divertidos.

Maine Lobster Dinner

Un plato de langosta de Maine

Mt. Katahdin is a favorite place for Mainers. In the summer they enjoy hiking in Mt. Katahdin and canoeing in its rivers. In the winter Mainers practice snowmobiling, ice fishing, and skiing on the mountain.

El Monte Katahdin es uno de los lugares favoritos de los maineses. En el verano disfrutan de excursiones y navegan en canoa por sus ríos. En el invierno, los maineses practican esquí, pesca en el hielo y motonieve en el Monte Katahdin.

Mt. Katahdin at the Baxter State Park

Monte Katahdin en el Parque Estatal Baxter

Maine Today

Maine has been building ships since the 1800s. Today the state makes modern boats, submarines, and ships.

Maine, hoy

Maine ha construído barcos desde los años 1800. Hoy, el estado fabrica modernos barcos, lanchas y submarinos.

A Modern Ship Built in Maine

Barco moderno construído en Maine

Portland, Lewiston, Bangor, and Auburn are important cities in Maine. Augusta is the capital of the state.

Portland, Lewiston, Bangor y Auburn son ciudades importantes de Maine. Augusta es la capital del estado.

State Capitol in Augusta, Maine

Capitolio del estado en Augusta, Maine

Activity:

Let's Draw Maine's State Flower

The white pine cone and tassel became Maine's state flower in 1895.

Actividad:

Dibujemos la flor del estado de Maine

La piña y las agujas del pino blanco han sido la flor del estado de Maine desde 1895.

1

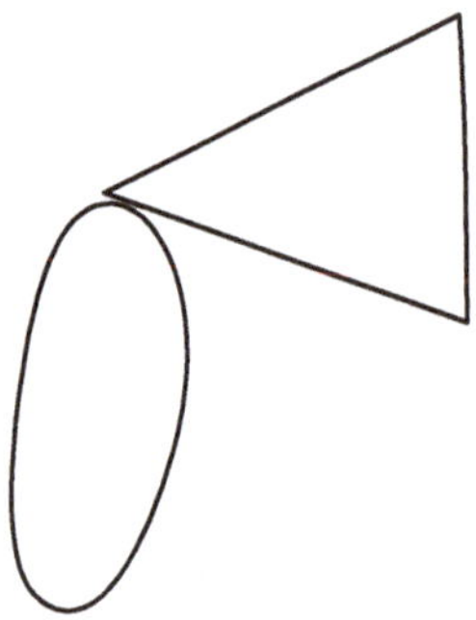

Start by drawing an oval. Then draw a triangle with its point touching the oval.

Comienza por trazar un óvalo. Luego dibuja un triángulo, con una de sus puntas tocando el óvalo.

2

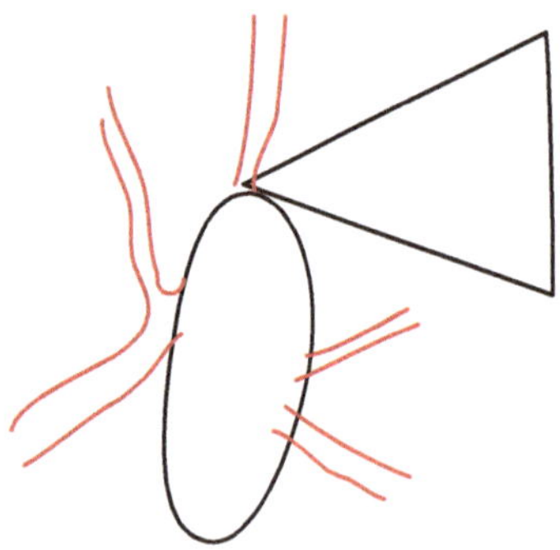

Now draw some of the branches you see in the photo behind the pinecone.

Ahora dibuja algunas de las ramas que están detrás de la piña, como ves en la foto.

3

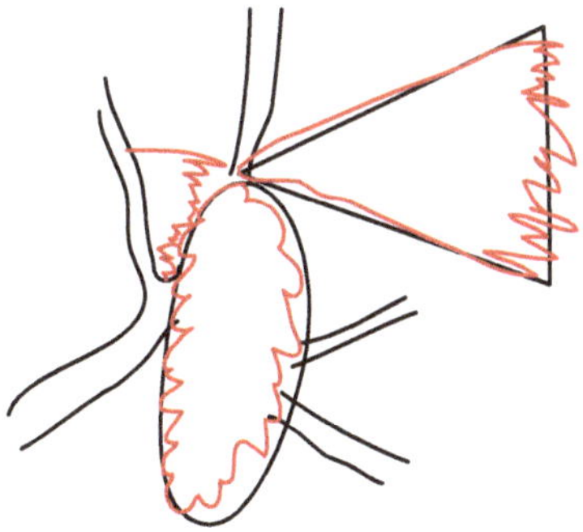

Draw the outline of the pinecone, and the bushy needles in the tassel. Use the guide drawn in step one.

Dibuja el contorno exterior de la piña y el grupo de agujas. Usa la guía que trazaste en el primer paso.

4

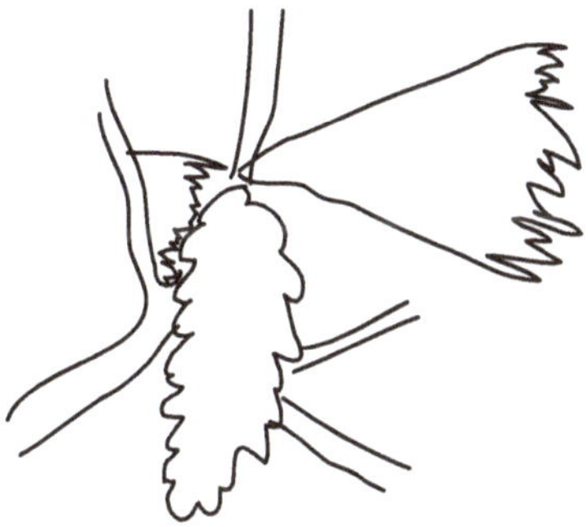

Erase all the guides drawn in the earlier steps.

Borra todos los trazos de guía que usaste en los primeros dos pasos.

5

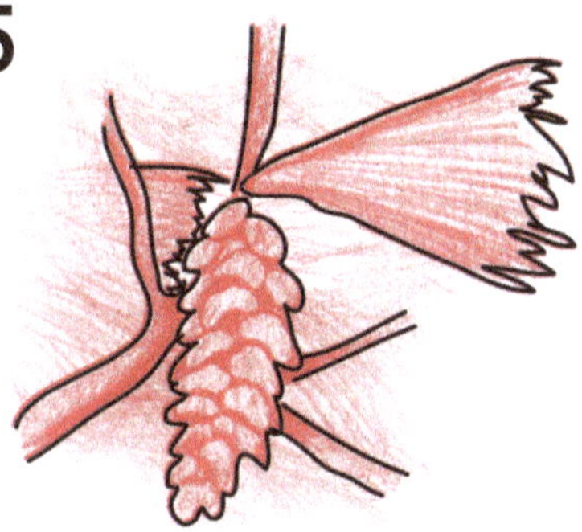

Add lines to make the scales of the pinecone. Shade the drawing.

Agrega líneas para dibujar las escamas de la piña. Sombrea el dibujo.

Timeline		Cronología
Giovanni da Verrazano becomes the first European explorer to visit Maine.	1524	Giovanni da Verrazano es el primer europeo en explorar Maine.
Maine's first government is established.	1636	Se establece el primer gobierno de Maine.
The first naval battle of the American Revolution is fought in Machias Bay, Maine.	1775	Se produce la primera batalla naval de la Revolución Americana en la Bahía Machias, Maine.
Maine's becomes the twenty-third state of the Union.	1820	Maine se convierte en el estado veintitrés de la Unión.
The Kennebec River floods Maine's capital Augusta.	1978	El Río Kennebeck inunda Augusta, la ciudad capital de Maine.
Penobscot and Passamaquoddy Indians win back 12.5 million acres (5.5 million hectares) of land taken from them at the eighteenth century.	1980	Las tribus Penobscot y Passamaquoddy recuperan 12.5 millones de acres (5.5 millones de hectáreas) que les habían sido arrebatados en el siglo dieciocho.

Maine Events	Eventos en Maine
January-February Winter activities in Bethel, Carrabasset Valley, and Jackman	Enero-febrero Actividades invernales, en Bethel, Carrabasset Valley y Jackman.
March Maine Maple Sunday	Marzo Domingo del azúcar de arce de Maine
June Acadian Festival at Madawaska Lobster Boat Races in Boothbay Harbor	Junio Festival Acadian, en Madawasa Carreras de barcos langosteros, en Boothbay Harbor
July Clam Festival in Yarmouth Potato Blossom Festival in Fort Fairfield	Julio Festival de la almeja, en Yarmouth Festival de la flor de la papa, en Fort Fairfield
August Lobsterfest in Rockland Maine Festival of the Arts in Portland	Agosto Festival de la langosta, en Rockland Festival de las Artes de Maine, en Portland
September Shipyard Cup in Boothbay Harbor	Septiembre Copa Astillero, en Boothbay Harbor
October Fall Foliage Festival in Boothbay Railway Village	Octubre Festival del follaje otoñal, en Boothbay Railway Village
December Christmas in Kennebunk	Diciembre Navidad, en Kennebuck

Maine Facts/Datos sobre Maine

Population
1.2 million

Población
1.2 millones

Capital
Augusta

Capital
Augusta

State Motto
Dirigo

Lema del estado
Yo guío

State Flower
White pinecone and tassel

Flor del estado
Piña y agujas del pino blanco

State Bird
Chickadee

Ave del estado
Carbonero

State Nickname
Pine Tree State

Mote del estado
El Estado del Pino

State Tree
Eastern white pine

Árbol del estado
Pino blanco oriental

State Song
"State of Maine Song"

Canción del estado
"Canción del estado de Maine"

Famous Mainers/Maineses famosos

Dorothea Lynde Dix
(1802–1887)
Educator
Educadora

Henry W. Longfellow
(1807–1882)
Poet
Poeta

Hannibal Hamlin
(1809–1891)
U.S. vice president
Vicepresidente de los E.U.A.

Nelson A. Rockefeller
(1908–1979)
U.S. vice president
Vicepresidente de los E.U.A.

Stephen King
(1947–)
Author
Escritor

Liv Tyler
(1977–)
Actress
Actriz

Words to Know/Palabras que debes saber

banner
banda

border
frontera

harbor
puerto

submarine
submarino

Here are more books to read about Maine:
Otros libros que puedes leer sobre **Maine**:

In English/En inglés:

Maine
America the Beautiful
Second Series
by Kent, Deborah
Children's Press , 1999

My First Book About Maine
by Marsh, Carole and
Zimmer, Kathy
Gallopade International, 2000

Words in English: 333

Palabras en español: 347

Index

Índice